IMAGES OF
SPORT

CARDIFF CITY
FOOTBALL CLUB
1971-1993

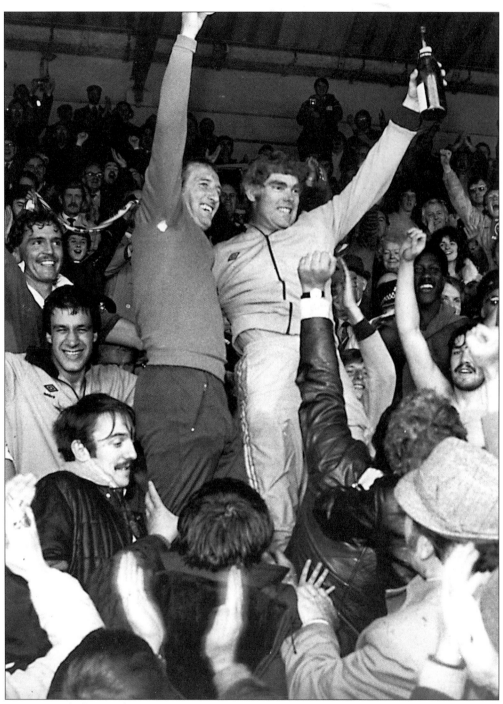

Jimmy Goodfellow and Len Ashurst celebrate promotion to Division Two after the 2-0 home win over Leyton Orient on 7 May 1983. Also in the photograph are Phil Dwyer, Roger Gibbins, Dave Bennett and Linden Jones. But, as with all of City's promotions since the mid-1970s, the success was short-lived.

STADIA

IMAGES OF
SPORT

CARDIFF CITY
FOOTBALL CLUB
1971-1993

RICHARD SHEPHERD

Acknowledgements

If no photographers had sat behind the goal-line in all weather, taking action shots of Cardiff City's matches, then there would be no archive photograph books on the club. In addition, no book of this nature would be complete without a number of off-field scenes to reflect the life of the club.

The 1971 to 1993 period is comparatively near enough in historical terms for all the material taken in that time to be still available, and did not take a great deal of finding, with much of it coming from my own extensive archive on Welsh football.

The *Western Mail and Echo* were kind enough to allow me to use several photographs and press-cuttings from the period covered by this book, and I am grateful to photographers Glyn Paul, Bob Reed and Terry Downey, who were covering the club during that time, for allowing me to use selections from their work. I am also grateful to Arthur Emery-Jones for unrestricted access to, and use of, the comprehensive Purchiss Collection.

My thanks to Harry Parsons for his foreword – I can think of no better person to have done it than 'H', who was the life and soul of the club for a thirty-year period that includes the years covered by this book.

Tempus Publishing and their commissioning editor James Howarth have been a great source of encouragement and their original format of football club archive photograph publications all over the country has proved a great success. I am pleased to have led the way with the first Cardiff City archive photograph book in 1996.

Last, but not least, my special thanks and appreciation to Brenda, without whose unfailing support and work on the project, I would never have achieved the deadline required for this publication.

Richard Shepherd
June 2000

Front cover: Dave Bennett (with Jeff Hemmerman) celebrates City's opening goal of the 1982/83 Third Division promotion season against Wrexham at Ninian Park.

First published 2000
STADIA edition 2007

STADIA is an imprint of
Tempus Publishing Limited
The Mill, Brimscombe Port,
Stroud, Gloucestershire, GL5 2QG
www.tempus-publishing.com

British Library Cataloguing in Publication Data.
A catalogue record for this book is available from the British Library.

ISBN 978 07524 2068 4

Typesetting and origination by Tempus Publishing Limited.
Printed in Great Britain.

Contents

Acknowledgements   4

Foreword   6

Introduction   7

1. On the Slide: 1971-1975   9

2. Alston to Ashurst: 1975-1982   23

3. One Up, Two Down and Division Four: 1982-1986   55

4. The Frank Burrows Era: 1986-1990   75

5. Wright is Watching Us: 1990-1993   95

Cardiff-born Harry Parsons – known to generations of City players as 'H' – is one of the great characters in Cardiff City's history. He watched the club as a boy in the late 1920s and well remembers going to see the 1927 FA Cup winners return from Wembley. He was a regular follower from then on, especially in the years following his return from overseas wartime service. In the mid-1960s, when he was connected with The Cardiff Central Boys Club, coaching and organising their teams, City manager Jimmy Scoular asked him to work for the club on a part-time basis. He became a full-time employee in August 1969 and over the years has been jack of all trades around the dressing room – kit manager, scout, youth team trainer and so on. During his thirty-year connection with the club, he travelled all over Europe with City. Harry sadly passed away in 2006.

Foreword

I spent thirty years behing the scene at Cardiff City, so I know everyone who has been included in this great book, and I could tell you a few stories about nearly all of them, but I won't because there might be a few divorces flying about!

What I will say is that I got on great with everyone at the club during my time there – managers, directors, players and other staff – and whenever I go to matches at Ninian Park these days, if any former players come there with the visiting clubs, they always make a point of finding me. When Ronnie Moore came two seasons ago as manager of Rotherham, he didn't bother to supervise his team's warm-up, he stayed inside with me to talk over old times – I reminded him that he never could score any goals with us!

Every picture in this book brings back memories to me – there are players shown who I found locally – Peter Sayer, David and Paul Giles, Tarki Micallef and Phil Dwyer to name but a few.

There are photographs of games that I remember so well, such as the night at Bury in May 1976 when we promotion and away matches when I had a few stories to tell about what happened to certain players at the hotel the previous night. My only regret is that my old mate Dr Leslie Hamilton died in early June, a couple of months before this book was published. He was the club's medical officer and then the consultant for thirty-five years until his death, and he came to the club around the time that the late Jimmy Scoular took me on. The Doc and I travelled all over Europe with Cardiff City and we had some good times together. He would have enjoyed reminiscing with me over this book by Richard Shepherd, who has done a great job in putting it together.

I'm sure all fans who have been following the club for years will enjoy this book as I've done – I look at pictures of Jimmy Scoular, who died a few years ago, and think of the memorable times we had, as I did with all the managers I worked for. I've got great memories of my years with Cardiff City and this book brings it all back to me.

'H'
July 2000

Born in Porthcawl, Richard Shepherd has been broadcasting on Welsh football since 1973. His connections with Cardiff City in fact go back to the 'Riverside' days of the club when one of his relatives played for that organisation. Richard began watching City in 1955 and covered them extensively during his twenty-three years with BBC Wales. He has since worked in independent radio, commentating on football, and has been editor of, and contributed to, Cardiff City's match programme.

Introduction

This is the third, and for the time being the last, of the trilogy of archive photograph books that I have compiled on Cardiff City Football Club. The next one, from 1993 onwards, must wait until a suitable time has elapsed. The period from 1971 to 1993 is far enough in the past to provide archive views but near enough for many supporters of the club to relate to the players, matches and personalities contained in these pages.

After the European glory years of the 1960s and early '70s, and the triple promotion challenge of 1968 to 1971, things began to fall apart for City. They were unable to compete with clubs that went on to higher things and Ninian Park, which had once regularly held 60,000 for international matches, began to deteriorate in the mid-1970s without the finances to improve the spectator facilities. At one stage, the capacity was authorised at just 10,000 before remedial work was carried out.

On the field, City fell out of the old Second Division in 1985 and since then have yet to play above the lower divisions. However, supporters of the club, which represents the capital city of Wales, still believe that Cardiff City should be playing at the highest level and would attract the support to sustain it.

Five relegations and four promotions in the twenty-two years covered by this book mean that City have never been able to capitalise on brief successes. Their best opportunity appeared to be in 1993 when, under Rick Wright's influence, they won the Third Division championship and the Welsh Cup, and were attracting the best crowds in the lower divisions. That is as far as this particular book travels, but recalled in these pages are most of the names who were familiar between 1971 and 1993.

This is not a detailed history of the club, which has already been chronicled by John Crooks in 1992. However, as with my previous publications on the club (covering 1899-1947 and 1947-1971), I have presented photographs in a chronological order to trace the course of Cardiff City over twenty-two years, and to remind fans of many of the players, managers, staff and matches along the way.

Richard Shepherd
June 2000

7

Two major names in the Cardiff City story between 1971 and 1993 were defender Phil Dwyer (left), and manager Frank Burrows (below). Locally-born Dwyer holds the club record with a total of 573 first team appearances (471 League games and 102 in various cup competitions). He was with the club from 1968, when he joined them as an apprentice, having been a Welsh schoolboy international, until March 1985 when he joined Rochdale – a total of seventeen years at Ninian Park. Mainly a full-back or central defender during his City career, he also played in midfield and in attack. He played for Wales at under-23, under-21 and senior levels, making 10 full appearances for his country, including at Ninian Park against England in 1978 when he played in attack and scored. He made his first team debut in October 1972 and almost lost his life playing for The Bluebirds when he choked after a collision with a Gillingham player in November 1975. Fortunately, he survived to become one of the most loyal players in the club's history. After his playing career, he joined South Wales Police.

When Scottish-born Frank Burrows became manager of Cardiff City in May 1986, the club had just completed a disastrous plunge from the Second to the Fourth Division in just two seasons. There was little or no money available for the former Raith, Scunthorpe and Swindon defender, but he had plenty of coaching and managerial experience with Swindon (coach), Portsmouth (coach and manager) and Sunderland (coach), and he began his team-building with free transfers, including former Wales international Alan Curtis from Southampton. The club did reasonably well in its first Fourth Division season (1986/87), and Frank Burrows was able to build on that foundation for 1987/88 by bringing several more astute signings including striker Jimmy Gilligan who cost a modest £17,500 from Lincoln City. By the end of the season, City had won promotion in second place and also took the Welsh Cup, gaining entry into the European Cup Winners' Cup. However, the finance was not there to take the club onwards and in late August 1989, Frank Burrows resigned, returning to Portsmouth as assistant-manager, later becoming manager. He was to return to Cardiff City in February 1998 and took the club to promotion from Division Three in 1999, becoming the only manager in the club's League history to win promotion in two different spells.

One

On the Slide
1971-1975

City had finished third in Division Two at the end of 1970/71, three points off the two promotion positions. When Brian Clark put them 2-0 up by half-time against Burnley (top, a header; bottom, a shot) on 14 August 1971 in the opening League game of 1971/72 in front of 23,026 fans, another promising season looked in store. However, it finished 2-2 and City went on to struggle against relegation, escaping by just one point.

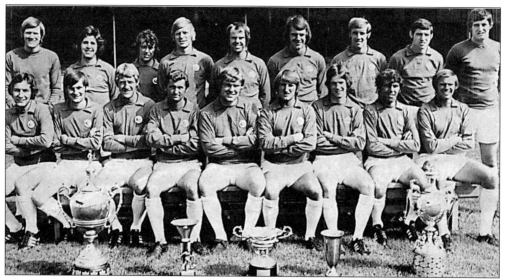

This was City's squad in late July 1971 with new signing Ken Jones, a full-back who cost £8,000 from Southampton. From left to right, back row: Frank Parsons, Nigel Rees, John Parsons, Richie Morgan, Ken Jones, Alan Warboys, Dave Carver, Mel Sutton, Jim Eadie. Front row: Steve Derrett, Leighton Phillips, Brian Clark, Peter King, Don Murray (captain), Ian Gibson, Freddie Pethard, Gary Bell, Bobby Woodruff. The Welsh Cup (bottom right) was on display as usual – City had won it for the fifth consecutive year in May 1971.

Two other 1971 summer signings were also made – wingers Alan Foggon (left) from Newcastle United for £25,000 and Tony Villars (right) who cost a nominal fee from Welsh League Panteg. Both Foggon, a former England youth international who left for Middlesbrough in October 1972, and Villars, who joined Newport County in July 1976, were talented players who underachieved during their time at Ninian Park.

City went out of the European Cup Winners' Cup in the first round to Dynamo Berlin. They drew the first leg 1-1 in East Germany and the second leg at Ninian Park on 29 September 1971 also finished 1-1 and went to penalties. Skipper Don Murray (seen here behind two Dynamo defenders) missed a vital spot-kick and City went out.

The highlight of the season was the FA Cup fifth round home tie against Don Revie's Leeds United, who beat City 2-0 and went on to win the cup. The attendance of 49,180 would be the last time a 40,000-plus crowd would be seen at Ninian Park. Here, Alan Foggon beats Leeds' Paul Madeley with Gary Bell watching. In the background is The Bob Bank.

City battled hard against Leeds who were second in Division One, and after Johnny Giles had put them ahead, Brian Clark (above) almost equalised, beating Gary Sprake with this effort that was narrowly wide. Giles (below), second from the right, settled the match just before time with this goal. The City players are Dave Carver (2) and Leighton Phillips (6) with Billy Irwin, signed from Irish club Bangor during October 1971, in goal. The Leeds players are Allan Clarke (8) and Mick Jones (9). Both photographs show the main stand before its extension in 1973.

The 1971/72 season was a contrasting one for these two players. Roger Hoy (left), signed from Luton in mid-August 1971 for £20,000, suffered a knee injury in early October and did not play again that season. Brian Clark (right) was top scorer for the third consecutive season.

The only acquisition in summer 1972 was twenty-one-year-old Irish defender Albert Larmour, signed from Linfield for £10,000 in July. Watching him sign are, from the left: City secretary Graham Keenor, the Linfield secretary and City manager Jimmy Scoular.

City were soon struggling in the early stages of 1972/73 and by mid-October three new names had been brought in. Defender Dave Powell (above left) and winger Gil Reece (above right), both Welsh internationals, came from Sheffield United on 21 September 1972 in exchange for Alan Warboys. Midfielder Johnny Vincent (below) came from Middlesbrough for £35,000 on 12 October and two days later scored on his debut in a 2-0 home win against his previous club! He is seen here in action against Preston at Ninian Park a fortnight later.

Executive changes at Ninian Park in October and November 1972. Former Swansea City chairman David Goldstone (above left) joined the board on 9 October 1972 and took over as chairman a few weeks later from Fred Dewey (above right). Mr Dewey, a Welsh international in the early 1930s, remained on the board as president, even after resigning with his son Viv in November 1973: he had been a director for eighteen years. He died in January 1980 having been with the club for twenty-five years.

Administration changes were also made, with secretary Graham Keenor (left), son of Wembley skipper Fred Keenor, resigning on 10 November 1972 after a twenty-year link with the club as junior player and administrator. He was replaced by assistant-secretary and former player Lance Hayward (right).

There were still problems on the field, despite the signings of striker Andy McCulloch (left) from QPR for £45,000 on 26 October and winger Willie Anderson (right) from Aston Villa on 20 February for £65,000.

A 4-1 home win over Huddersfield on 21 April 1973 as Andy McCulloch scores one of his two goals. The victory eventually kept City in Division Two on goal average and Huddersfield went down.

A new name and new facilities in July 1973. Midfield player George Smith (left) is signed by Jimmy Scoular from Birmingham City for £50,000 and the Main Stand extensions on the Sloper Road side of Ninian Park are completed (right). The Grange End covered terrace is still there.

Cardiff City's squad for 1973/74. From left to right, back row: George Smith, Johnny Vincent, Albert Larmour, Peter King, Richard Morse, Bill Irwin, Willie Anderson, Roger Hoy, Andy McCulloch, Peter Morgan. Front row: Phil Dwyer, Dave Powell, Richie Morgan, Gary Bell, Don Murray (captain), Freddie Pethard, Leighton Phillips, Bobby Woodruff, Gil Reece. The two large trophies are the South Wales Senior Cup and the Welsh Cup. Also there are the S.A. Brain Trophy and various pieces of silverware won by the youth team.

Sporting Lisbon of Portugal were back at Ninian Park on 19 September 1973, for the first round first leg of the Cup Winners' Cup, for the first time since December 1964. Don Murray and Vitor Damas meet before a 0-0 draw. City were unbeaten in their opening eight League and Cup games, but then struggled for the rest of the season.

On 22 November 1973, Leicester winger John Farrington (left) telephoned to say he would sign for City: the fee was a club record £60,000. On the same day City signed the very talented Notts County midfielder Willie Carlin (right) for £10,000. Carlin retired at the end of that season having helped City stay up.

In mid-November 1973, former Manchester United Manager Frank O'Farrell (left) replaced Jimmy Scoular. The ex-Republic of Ireland international, seen here with Miss Bluebird 1973/74 Lynne Jones, only stayed until April before taking up an offer in Iran. His replacement was Jimmy Andrews (far right), who O'Farrell had brought in from Tottenham as his coach.

Manchester City goalkeeper Ron Healey was signed on loan in mid-March 1974 and was then signed permanently. He remained with Cardiff City until 1982 after becoming a Republic of Ireland international, eventually retiring through injury.

It was looking like the drop for City in mid-April 1974 when they lost 2-1 at Nottingham Forest, despite taking the lead through this goal from Johnny Vincent.

It was between City and Crystal Palace for relegation in the final match of 1973/74 at Ninian Park. A 1-1 draw in front of 26,781 was enough to keep City up and send Palace down, with this memorable equaliser from Tony Villars.

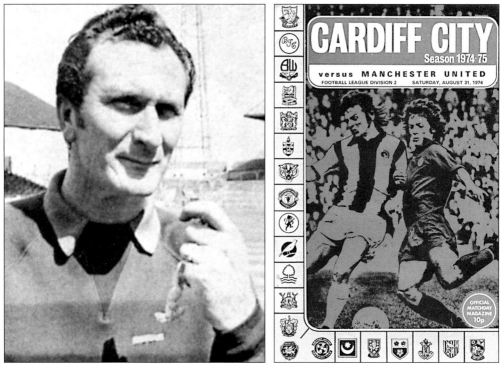

Reserve team coach Ken Whitfield (left) arrived from Luton Town in July 1974, while Manchester United arrived for a Second Division match in late August (right). They had just been relegated, but Cardiff were the ones who went down that season. They have never met since these 1974/75 encounters in a competitive match.

One of City's best signings of the 1970s came from Northampton Town for £30,000 in mid-October 1974. Scottish-born John Buchanan, seen here in action against Nottingham Forest a month later, was a hard-shooting midfield player who spent seven years at Ninian Park.

Two well-known names left during the season. Defender Don Murray (left) joined Hearts in November 1974 after twelve years at Ninian Park and full-back Gary Bell (right) went to Newport County in January 1975 after almost nine years with City.

During the latter half of 1974/75, City's wives, girlfriends and office staff formed their own ladies team. From left to right, back row: Julie Cole (commercial office), Tricia Parsons (niece of kit manager Harry Parsons), Christa Pope (office staff), Vera Anderson (wife of Willie), Eileen Skinner, Shirley Deans. Front row: Hazel Hobbs (fiancée of Jimmy McInch), Maureen Smith (wife of George), Carol Reece (wife of Gil), Jane Buchanan (wife of John), Sylvia McDonald.

Two

Alston to Ashurst
1975-1982

Following City's relegation to Division Three, a new consortium took over from David Goldstone in the summer of 1975. From left to right: Dewi Evans, Jim Jarvis, Clive Griffiths, Stefan Terlezki (chairman), Julius Hermer, 'Tiny' Latner, Eddie Jones, Welsh actor and comedian Stan Stennett. Tony Clemo (vice-chairman), Jack Leonard and Bob Grogan were also on the new board. Leonard and Grogan ran a civil engineering firm called Kenton Utilities and were to play a major role in the club's affairs during the next ten years.

Returning to Ninian Park in the summer of 1975 was former City striker Brian Clark (left), who had been with AFC Bournemouth and Millwall during the previous three years, while joining from Blackpool was striker Tony Evans (right). Both are shown here soon after their arrival.

A pre-season golf session at the Glamorganshire Club with assistant-manager and coach Ken Whitfield showing the way. From left to right: Gil Reece, Brian Attley, Ron Healey, Brian Clark, Clive Charles, Jimmy Andrews (manager), Derek Showers, David Giles, Phil Dwyer, Albert Larmour, John Buchanan.

A major signing arrives in mid-August 1975. Former Blackburn, Tottenham and Wales defender and captain Mike England signs an autograph for young City fan Marc Stafford shortly after his return from playing in the USA that summer. He had intended to retire, but Jimmy Andrews persuaded him to play one more season. Mike's experience and leadership were a vital factor in City's immediate promotion from Division Three. He returned to America at the end of the season and in 1980 became Wales' team manager.

Two more good signings as City's promotion challenge takes shape. Midfielder Doug Livermore (left) cost £20,000 from Norwich City on 21 August and striker Adrian Alston (right), a Preston-born 1974 World Cup Australian international, came from Luton for £25,000 in late October 1975 to form a dangerous goal-scoring partnership with Tony Evans.

The last signing of City's promotion squad came in early March 1976 when midfield player Alan Campbell (left) came from Birmingham for £20,000. Alan is seen here a month later with Tony Evans in a 1-0 home win over Chester.

Locally-born winger/forward Peter Sayer (middle) was back in the squad in the latter half of 1975/76 after fracturing his ankle at the end of the previous season. Peter, seen here against Preston in a 1-0 home win on 7 April 1976, was to become a Welsh international the following year. He was later with Brighton, Preston, Chester and Northwich Victoria.

One of the great matches of 1975/76 when 35,549 saw a 2-0 home win for second-placed City over leaders Hereford United on 14 April 1976. Gil Reece breaks through, challenged by Roy Carter (left) and Dudley Tyler.

Promotion is secured as Adrian Alston (10) forces in the winner for a 1-0 victory at Bury on 4 May 1976. Thousands of City fans were amongst the 7,135 crowd in what was Mike England's last match for the club.

The promotion squad (except Mike England) in mid-May 1976. From left to right, back row: Freddie Pethard, Doug Livermore, Ron Healey, Brian Clark, Keith Pontin, Derek Showers, John Buchanan, Tony Villars, Willie Anderson, Albert Larmour, Phil Dwyer. Front row: David Giles, Peter Sayer, Richie Morgan, Tony Evans, Adrian Alston, Clive Charles, Alan Campbell, Brian Attley.

The end of a great season with a Welsh Cup final victory over Hereford United. The team are seen here with the trophy in the Ninian Park dressing room after the 3-2 second leg victory on 19 May 1976. Top left is Alan Sealey, the former West Ham forward, who scouted for the club during the season and joined the coaching staff in the summer of 1976.

After aggregate wins over Swiss club Servette of Geneva in the Cup Winner's Cup and Bristol Rovers in the League Cup in the first four games of 1976/77, City began their Second Division campaign with this 2-0 win against Charlton at The Valley on 21 August 1976. Derek Showers (9) scored twice, but not this time as Charlton defender Bob Curtis clears, watched by Willie Anderson.

By early October 1976, City were out of the Cup Winners' Cup, losing to Dynamo Tblisi, and were in the bottom three of Division Two. So, on 7 October Jimmy Andrews got busy and brought in defender Paul Went (left) from Portsmouth for £25,000, and winger Steve Grapes (right) from Norwich City for £7,500 on 19 October.

The most controversial signing came on 30 December 1976 with the arrival of the talented but self-destructive striker Robin Friday from Reading for £25,000. He was to spend a turbulent twelve months with the club. Friday replaced Adrian Alston, who went to Tampa Bay Rowdies twelve days earlier. Friday was to leave the club and football exactly twelve months later. On 31 December 1990, he was found dead in unexplained circumstances at his Ealing flat. He was thirty-eight years old.

Friday (10) scored twice on his City debut in this 3-0 home win over Fulham on 1 January 1977 in front of 20,268. Here, John Buchanan (middle) opens the scoring.

A week later 27,868 fans saw Peter Sayer make national football headlines with this goal in City's 1-0 FA Cup third round home win over Tottenham Hotspur.

A dramatic 3-2 home win over Wrexham in round four and another large crowd of 28,953. John Buchanan (far right) scores an injury-time winner seconds after Wrexham had come back from 2-1 down to make it 2-2.

The FA Cup run finished in round five with a 2-1 home defeat by Everton in front of 35,582, despite City taking a first-half lead through this goal from Tony Evans.

Robin Friday's on- and off-field behaviour often caused the club problems. He scored twice in this 4-2 home win over Luton on 16 April 1977 and let Milija Aleksic know his feelings after one of his goals, following an earlier foul on him by the Luton 'keeper. City missed relegation on goal average that season.

One of the highlights of an undistinguished 1977/78 season was this 3-1 home win on 24 September over Fulham, who included former Manchester United and Northern Ireland international George Best, seen here being tackled by John Buchanan.

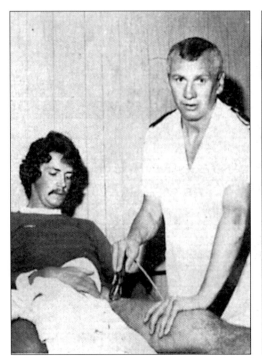 

Behind the scenes there was a new club physiotherapist for 1977/78 with former Welsh Guardsman Tudor Jones (left) coming from Cardiff Royal Infirmary. He is seen here treating Freddie Pethard. Meanwhile, kit manager Harry Parsons (right) kept the apprentices in order with his own special award every Friday lunchtime.

The side continued to struggle on the field and on 31 October 1977, Welsh international full-back Rod Thomas was signed by Jimmy Adams from Derby County for £10,000.

The end of the Grange End under the Safety of Sports Ground Act, which at one stage of 1977/78 reduced the ground's capacity to 10,000 by order of the local authority. The fifty-year-old cover and wooden terracing had to come down. *Above:* As it looked behind Albert Larmour on 31 December 1977 against Charlton. *Below:* As it looked behind Rod Thomas against Crystal Palace on 8 April 1978.

Newcastle United midfield player Mickey Burns was signed as player-coach by Jimmy Andrews on 2 August 1978 for a club record £75,000 (left). The former Skelmersdale and Blackpool player only had a brief spell at Ninian Park, making just 9 League and cup appearances, including this one against Cambridge United (right) at Ninian Park on 9 September. Three weeks later he joined Middlesbrough for £75,000.

Two more newcomers. On 15 August 1978 Welsh international defender Dave Roberts (left) came from Hull City for £50,000. Dave is seen here on his City debut against Preston at Ninian Park on 11 August. A few days later John Lewis (right) gave up his job with British Steel to become a full-time professional. Assistant-manager Ken Whitfield, seen here with him, had spotted the midfielder playing against City's Welsh League side for Pontllanfraith the previous season.

Striker Gary Stevens (left) was signed from West Midlands club Evesham United on 6 September 1978 for £3,000. The former Hereford maintenance fitter is in action at Ninian Park against Blackburn in a 2-0 win on 23 September, when he scored his first goal for the club.

From player to manager. Long-serving defender Richie Morgan (left) took over as acting manager from Jimmy Andrews in early November 1978 and was appointed full manager a month later. Richie, seen here against Notts County in one of his final first team games in 1976/77, had since been helping the youngsters in reserve team matches.

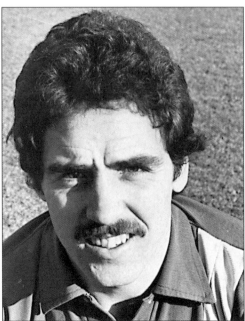

Locally-born ex-apprentice striker Constantinous 'Tarki' Micellef (left) made his City debut on 16 December 1978 at Sheffield United. He was with the club until 1983, when he joined Newport County, and was later at Gillingham before returning to Ninian Park in 1984/85. Full-back Colin Sullivan (right) came from Norwich City for £60,000 in late-January 1979. He later played for Portsmouth and Swansea.

This was one match in which Ronnie Moore did score – against Brighton at Ninian Park on 14 April 1979. The big striker cost £110,000 from Tranmere on 22 February 1979 but, despite his non-stop efforts, scored only 6 goals in 56 League games before going in August 1980 to Rotherham United where his goal-touch returned.

Former Everton and City defender Brian Harris returned to Ninian Park in February 1979 as coach together with ex-Bangor City boss Dave Elliott, appointed as assistant-manager, and ex-player Bobby Woodruff, who took charge of the club's Welsh League side and coached City's associate schoolboys.

City finished ninth in Division Two at the end of 1978/79 after being unbeaten in their final eleven games. This was one of them – a 1-1 home draw against Burnley on 5 May as former Cheltenham forward Ray Bishop, signed in January 1977, goes near. In the background is the rebuilt and now uncovered Grange End.

City's line-up at the start of 1979/80 with Doug Livermore returning on the coaching staff after playing out his career at Chester. From left to right, back row: John Lewis, Dave Roberts, Keith Pontin, Ronnie Moore, John Davies, Ron Healey, Gary Stevens, Rod Thomas, Alan Campbell, John Buchanan. Front row: Brian Harris (assistant-manager), Steve Grapes, Billy Ronson, Phil Dwyer (captain), Richie Morgan (manager), Colin Sullivan, Ray Bishop, Linden Jones, Doug Livermore (coach).

Hard work on The Wenallt in early July 1979 as Rod Thomas, Phil Dwyer and Gary Stevens take a breather in pre-season training after running up the mountain near Caerphilly.

In June 1979 apprentice Paul Giles (left), the younger brother of former City forward David Giles, became a full professional, while the following month Blackpool midfielder Billy Ronson (right) was signed for £135,000.

City's first win of 1979/80. Gary Stevens (8) heads the only goal of the game against QPR at Ninian Park on 22 August. Stevens was with City until June 1982 when he moved to Shrewsbury Town.

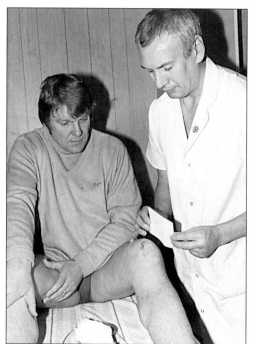

Don Murray (left) was back at Ninian Park in mid-September 1979 as part-time player-coach to City's Welsh League team. A few years off the field meant that he needed physiotherapist Tudor Jones's services. The start of October saw former West Bromwich Albion midfielder Wayne Hughes (right) signed from Tulsa Roughnecks (USA) for a £70,000 fee.

After an absence of fourteen years, League matches with Swansea resumed following their 1979 promotion. City lost 2-1 at the Vetch Field on 1 January 1980 despite taking the lead through John Lewis, seen here beating Jeremy Charles.

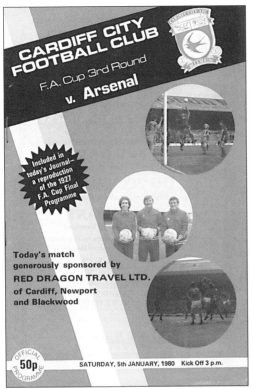

In the third round of the FA Cup, holders Arsenal were the visitors at Ninian Park. Despite the efforts of top scorer Ray Bishop (right), City were held 0-0 in front of 21,972. Ronnie Moore (below) beats Arsenal's Willie Young but his header was saved by Pat Jennings. City lost 2-1 in the replay at Highbury.

On 7 April 1980, Swansea City were defeated 1-0 at Ninian Park in their first League visit since 1965. Billy Ronson is seen here scoring the winner, his first goal since mid-October. From left to right: Tommy Craig (Swansea), Gary Stevens (City), Wyndham Evans (Swansea).

Easter 1980 saw City's youth squad compete once again in an international youth tournament at Roubaix, northern France. The group are seen here before their departure. From left to right, back row: Doug Livermore (manager). David Haskell, Neil Baldock, Mark Willetts, Mario Anzani, Paul Davies, Dean Piper, Ian Turner, Harry Parsons (kit manager/trainer). Front row: Steve James, Mike Lewis, Paul Giles, Andrew Wood, Paul Miller, Martin Thomas, Paul Maddy, Andrew Dyson.

One win in their final six games saw City finish in the lower half of the table. They lost this match 1-0 at home to West Ham United on 19 April 1980. Steve Grapes is seen here in a challenge with Alan Devonshire. The east London club beat Arsenal in the FA Cup final a few weeks later.

On 2 May 1980, former British Olympic sprinter and captain Ron Jones (centre) was appointed Cardiff City's general manager/secretary after four years at Queen's Park Rangers. Here he is on the day of his City appointment at Ninian Park with chairman Bob Grogan and team manager Richie Morgan.

On 18 May 1980, City's Welsh under-21 defender Keith Pontin (right) won his first senior cap, playing in this 4-1 win over England at Wrexham. The Wales goalkeeper is Dai Davies of Wrexham. Keith, who had been an ever-present for City from mid-September 1979 to the end of the season, was an ex-apprentice who had signed as a professional in May 1974. The Pontyclun-born defender left City for Merthyr in the summer of 1983.

City's squad look confident in early August 1980, but they would avoid relegation only on goal difference. From left to right, back row: Mark Elliott, Keith Pontin, Kevin Davies, Wayne Hughes, Dave Roberts. Middle row: Tudor Jones (physiotherapist), Doug Livermore (youth coach), Paul Maddy, Paul Davies, Phil Dwyer, Gary Stevens, Peter Grotier, Ron Healey, John Lewis, Rod Thomas, Andrew Wood, John Buchanan, Brian Harris (assistant manager). Front row: Linden Jones, Tarki Micallef, Alan Campbell, Steve Grapes, Richie Morgan (team manager), Billy Ronson, Ray Bishop, Colin Sullivan, Paul Giles.

Two additions for the 1980/81 season. Striker Peter Kitchen (left) was signed by Richie Morgan from Fulham on 20 August for £100,000. Cwmcarn-born apprentice midfield player Paul Maddy (right) signed full professional forms and was to make his debut in mid-September 1980. Former Doncaster and Orient player Kitchen would be top scorer that season.

In mid-October 1980, full-back Linden Jones (left), a former apprentice who had played several games since his February 1979 debut, established himself at right-back until his move to Newport County in September 1983. Mid-November saw an impressive debut for young Paul Giles (right).

The match against Luton on 22 November 1980 saw the visit of former Prime Minister, James (now Lord) Callaghan (left), the MP for City's constituency, who presented a Football Grounds Improvement Trust cheque for £97,000 to chairman Bob Grogan. That month also saw the departure of Doug Livermore (right) who joined Norwich City as reserve team coach.

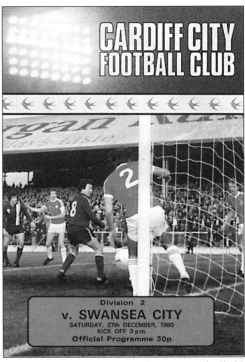

Well-known names and well-remembered games. Manchester City legend Tony Book (left) joined City's coaching staff in November 1980 and on 27 December came a 3-3 home draw with promotion-chasing Swansea City.

Gary Stevens gives City a twelfth-minute lead against Swansea in front of a 21,269 crowd. From left to right: Peter Kitchen, Stevens, unknown, Nigel Stevenson (Swansea), Phil Dwyer.

Above: The goal which City fans still remember – John Buchanan's 35-yard shot (or was it 40 yards?) from a Wayne Hughes tapped free-kick leaves Swansea 'keeper Dave Stewart helpless. City came back from 3-1 down to level at 3-3. *Below:* On 18 April 1981, City held Division One-bound Swansea 1-1 at the Vetch Field with this late header from Peter Kitchen (centre).

City were in danger of the drop with two 1980/81 games to go. *Left:* A 0-0 draw against Derby at home on 2 May as Gary Stevens challenges 'keeper Roger Jones. *Right:* Another 0-0 draw against already-promoted West Ham on 6 May to avoid relegation on goal average as Tarki Micallef beats Alvin Martin. However, it was only delaying the inevitable…

The squad in late July 1981 at the start of a season which would end in relegation. Included in this group are new trainer/coach Colin Prophett from Crewe, forward Paul Sugrue signed from Manchester City that summer and full-back Tim Gilbert, who had come from Sunderland in February 1981. From left to right: Woodruff (youth team coach), Kitchen, Thomas, Hughes, Healey, Grotier, Davies, Pontin, Stevens, Prophett (coach). Middle row: Lewis, Grapes, Dwyer, Morgan (manager), Ronson, Gilbert, Sullivan. Front row: Jones, Maddy, Micallef, Sugrue, Buchanan, Giles.

On 9 September 1981, City signed defender Gary Bennett from Manchester City on a free transfer and three days later signed his elder brother Dave, a striker, from the Maine Road club for £125,000. This is a rare photograph of both of them in action – Dave (centre) and Gary (6). The game was a 1-0 home win over Derby on 4 December 1981.

Former West Bromwich and Wales full-back Graham Williams (left) was appointed team coach in early-November 1981, with Richie Morgan becoming general manager. In January 1982, City's former Welsh international winger and ex-director George Edwards (right) returned to the board after an absence of nearly seven years.

On 3 March 1982, with City having collected just one point from eight games and near the foot of the table, Len Ashurst replaced Graham Williams and Richie Morgan. The former Newport County manager is seen here just after his appointment with some of City's staff, including Harry Parsons.

Dave Bennett hits the winner in a 2-1 home victory over Orient on 10 April 1982 as City showed a gradual improvement with several newcomers.

The 1981/82 end-of-season squad with several new names. They reached the Welsh Cup final, losing on aggregate to Swansea City. From left to right, back row: Jimmy Mullen (on loan from Rotherham), Mick Henderson (signed from Watford), Wayne Hughes, Gary Stevens, Ron Healey, Gary Bennett, Keith Pontin, Peter Kitchen. Front row: John Lewis, Paul Maddy, Andy Polycarpou (ex-Cambridge United), Dave Bennett, Tarki Micallef, Steve Grapes, Linden Jones, Alan Sanders.

Dave Bennett's shot is blocked by Luton's 'keeper Jake Findlay in the final League game of the season on 17 May 1982. City lost 3-2 to the Second Division champions and failed to avoid relegation by two points.

Three

One Up, Two Down and Division Four
1982-1986

City's Division Three squad for 1982/83 with several new names. From left to right, back row: Roger Gibbins (Cambridge United), Andrew Dibble, Martin Thomas (on loan from Bristol Rovers), David Tong (Shrewsbury), Middle row: Harry Parsons (kit manager), Jeff Hemmerman (Portsmouth), Keith Pontin, Gary Bennett, Paul Maddy, Bobby Woodruff (youth coach). Front row: John Lewis, Tarki Micallef, Len Ashurst (manager), Jimmy Mullen (Rotherham), Jimmy Goodfellow (ex-Newport County physiotherapist/coach), Dave Bennett, Linden Jones.

Dave Bennett equalises against Wrexham at Ninian Park on 28 August, the opening day of the 1982/83 season. Jeff Hemmerman is behind him. Although Wrexham won 2-1, it was City's only home League defeat of the season.

Billy Woof (left) came on trial from Middlesbrough in early September, scored the winner on his debut against Wigan in a 3-2 triumph, fell out with Len Ashurst and left after just one game! Godfrey Ingram (right) came from San Jose Earthquakes in mid-September 1982 for a reported £180,000. He rejoined the Earthquakes in late November for an identical fee. Was he on loan or was it a genuine transfer in and transfer out?

This Jeff Hemmerman header gave City a 1-0 home win over his former club Portsmouth on 30 October 1982 and put Len Ashurst's men into fourth place in Division Three.

Ashurst slams shameful City

THIS WAS City's most humiliating FA Cup defeat for 52 years, prompting manager Len Ashurst to break his usual rule of not criticising individual players.

He blamed John Lewis over Weymouth's first goal for "not tracking his man."

He blamed Phil Dwyer for the

By KARL WOODWARD   **Cardiff City 2, Weymouth 3**

second goal — "He had all the time in the world to clear the ball," and he blamed teenage 'keeper Andrew Dibble for Weymouth's match-winner.

"The third goal was pure farce. Jimmy Mullen was bending down tying his boot laces and told Dibble to hold on with his goal kick, but Andrew took it and miscued.

"It was schoolboy stuff from a professional team, and smacks of a complete lack of discipline. I don't usually pin criticism on individuals, but this time I have to. I don't have to sit on the bench and be

howled off by irate supporters because we have given away three goals. I can't accept that and I can't let players get away with it.

"I don't think the heavy state of the pitch is relevant at all. We were two up at half time and should have been home and dry."

City seemed to be coasting to victory when they established a two-goal lead after 36 minutes. Roger Gibbins, who had an excellent game up front as stand in for the Cup-tied Bob Hatton, gave City a 28-minute lead with a diving header after Dwyer had turned back a deep cross by Lewis.

A major shock in the FA Cup second round on 11 December 1982 and Len Ashurst did not hold back.

One of the most dramatic goals of the season as Jeff Hemmerman hits a late winner in front of a 15,972 Ninian Park crowd to beat Newport County 3-2 on 27 December 1982. Watching are Terry Boyle (left) and Vaughan Jones, both later to play for City.

A vital signing that season was experienced striker Bob Hatton (left) who came from Sheffield United on 1 December. Cwmbran-born ex-apprentice 'keeper Andy Dibble (right) played in most matches from mid-November. He had made his debut on his seventeenth birthday – 8 May 1982 – the previous season.

First against second at Fratton Park on 12 March as 24,350 see City hold leaders Portsmouth 0-0. Gary Bennett (left, white shirt) was inches wide with this close-range effort.

An Easter Monday 1-0 defeat at promotion rivals Newport County on 4 April. A 16,052 Somerton Park crowd look on as Phil Dwyer's header is pushed onto the post by 'keeper Mark Kendall (right). Newport went top, but failed to go up, while City did.

David Tong was almost ever-present during this season, but had not scored a League goal until this 3-0 home win against Doncaster on 9 April. He scored twice and this was his first.

A 3-1 home victory over Brentford on Bank Holiday Monday 3 May 1983, with Bob Hatton (9) scoring the second. This put City level on points with leaders Portsmouth with two games left. A home win against Orient the following Saturday would take City up. Part-timer Hatton, an insurance broker in Sheffield, retired at the end of the season as agreed with the club when he came in December.

The two goals against Orient on 7 May 1983 which took City back to Division Two. John Lewis (above) scores in the first half and Dave Bennett (below) seals it in the second. A crowd of 11,480 saw the game. City's promotion prospects had looked in doubt in early April 1983 when they had lost at Newport County and were out of the top three, following one victory in seven League games. However, from then on they went from strength to strength and were unbeaten in their remaining seven matches, winning five and drawing two. For Phil Dwyer, the season was particularly pleasing – City's long-serving defender had looked to be on his way out of Ninian Park before 1982/83 kicked off after a knee injury at the end of 1981/82 when he was given a free transfer by Len Ashurst. However, the manager offered him the chance to re-establish himself if he could fight his way back to full fitness. After a slow start to the season, Phil proved himself to be one of the mainstays of the season. Surprisingly for a promotion team, City used no fewer than five goalkeepers during the course of the season – triallist Steve Humphries from Doncaster Rovers, Martin Thomas on loan from Bristol Rovers, Andrew Dibble, Jim Brown on loan from Chesterfield and Eric Steele on loan from Watford. City finished as runners-up to Portsmouth, with Roger Gibbins the only player to appear in every League game and Jeff Hemmerman finished as top scorer with 27 in League and cup. For skipper Jimmy Mullen, it was the third time in his career that he had captained a promotion-winning team. Despite City's success, their average home League attendance was only 7,681, even though they lost at home only once in Division Three all season.

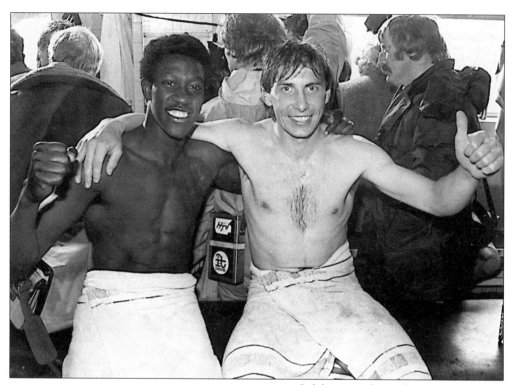

Celebrations for goalscorers Dave
Bennett and John Lewis in the
dressing room after the win over
Orient, but troubled times lay ahead.
In the final match at Bristol Rovers
a week later, Jeff Hemmerman (left)
badly damaged his knee-ligaments
and was eventually forced to retire.
The club's financial position was
giving cause for concern and during
the summer Bennett left for Coventry
City. In late August 1983 chairman
Bob Grogan resigned because of a
serious illness and less then a year
after promotion, manager Len Ashurst
left to join Sunderland. So, with
Dave Bennett, Jeff Hemmerman and
Bob Hatton all unavailable for the
following season, City were hardly
in a position to make the most of
their return to Division Two. It was
the second time in seven years that
City had regained Second Division
status at the first attempt, but they
were to begin 1983/84 with a weaker
squad than the one which had gained
promotion.

New shirts and new names in August 1983. From left to right, back row: Gary Bennett, Chris Roden (on loan from Brighton), Roger Gibbins, Andrew Dibble, Gary Plumley (from Newport County), Paul Evans, Phil Dwyer, Paul Bodin. Front row: Andy Crawford (from AFC Bournemouth), Wayne Matthews, John Lewis, Gordon Owen (from Sheffield Wednesday), Jimmy Mullen, Tarki Micallef, Linden Jones, David Tong.

Full-back Paul Bodin (3) was in his second season with City and he scored his first ever goals for the club in this 2-1 home win over Manchester City on 29 August 1983. This was his second, which won the match.

On the morning of that win over Manchester City, Bob Grogan (left), suffering from cancer, resigned as chairman with Jack Leonard (right) taking over. Ten days later, Bob Grogan died. He had joined the board in 1975 and his firm, Kenton Utilities of Newcastle, had saved the club from going out of business two years earlier. Irishman Leonard was managing director of Kenton Utilities.

In late September 1983, there was a five-player deal between City and Newport County. Into Ninian Park came Karl Elsey and Nigel Vaughan, seen here scoring in the 2-0 home win over Carlisle United on 8 October. Joining Newport were John Lewis, Tarki Micallef, and Linden Jones.

A match-winning debut for Trevor Lee (11). Signed from AFC Bournemouth three days before Christmas 1983, Lee headed this winner in a 3-2 home victory over Swansea City on Boxing Day. The 14,580 crowd was Ninian Park's best of the season.

On 11 February 1984, Jeff Hemmerman returned in this 1-0 home defeat against Leeds United following his knee injury the previous May, but was unable to recover his former sharpness. He left the club at the end of the season before returning as physiotherapist.

On 4 March 1983 Len Ashurst resigned to take over at Sunderland. City put skipper Jimmy Mullen and physiotherapist/coach Jimmy Goodfellow in temporary charge. Two months later, Goodfellow was named team manager with Mullen as player-coach.

Action from one of the most sensational Ninian Park games of 1983/84 as Roger Gibbins gives City the lead against eventual promotion winners Chelsea on 31 March. City were 3-0 ahead, but conceded three goals in the last six minutes to draw 3-3, with the equaliser coming from a hotly disputed penalty for handball against David Tong in the last minute.

A relegation campaign lay ahead in August 1984 and it was to be long-serving Phil Dwyer's last season with City. Four newcomers were brought in that summer. From left to right, back row: Karl Elsey, Roger Gibbins, Phil Dwyer, Gary Plumley, Lee Smelt (from Halifax), Colin Smith, David Grant, Paul Bodin. Front row: Vaughan Jones (from Newport County), David Tong, Jimmy Mullen (player-coach), Jimmy Goodfellow (team manager), Nigel Vaughan, Kevin Summerfield (from Walsall), John Seasman.

A surprise arrival in early September 1984 as a non-contract player was former England international Gerry Francis (left), who had recently been player-manager at Exeter. Another well-known name, who came in as manager at the end of September, was former Cardiff, Derby and Wales midfielder Alan Durban (right). The ex-Shrewsbury, Stoke and Sunderland manager took over from Jimmy Goodfellow.

Above: One of the brighter moments in a disastrous 1984/85 season as Phil Dwyer (4) heads a seventy-seventh minute winner in a 2-1 home victory over Leeds United on 12 September. *Below:* Gerry Francis (on right) played seven League games for City. This was the last one, against Portsmouth in a 2-1 home defeat on 6 October. Karl Elsey is seen here scoring City's goal.

Alan Durban brought in thirteen players during the course of that season, including transfers, loans and triallists. Amongst these were Welsh international midfielder Brian Flynn (left) from Burnley for £18,000 on 8 November and striker Graham Withey (right, no.10) from Coventry City just before Christmas.

Two other forwards brought in during November 1984 were Kevin Meacock (left) and Paul McLoughlin (right) who had both been playing for Devizes Town. They were Bristol-born players who had previously tried their luck in New Zealand with Gisbourne City.

This was Phil Dwyer's 573rd and last competitive appearance for Cardiff City, against Notts County at Ninian Park in a 4-1 defeat on 17 March 1985. Four days later he was transferred to Rochdale as City headed into Division Three.

Who's that number eight heading through the Oxford United defence on 6 April 1985 in a 2-0 home defeat? It's Dean Saunders on loan from Swansea City. Dean made 4 League appearances before going back and went on to have a great career with Brighton, Oxford, Derby, Liverpool, Aston Villa, Galatasaray, Nottingham Forest, Sheffield United, Benfica, Bradford City and Wales.

More new names for 1985/86 and there would be even more signings, but City were to go down again, into Division Four for the first time. This was the squad on 12 August 1985. From left to right, back row: Alan Durban (manager), Carlton Leonard (player/physiotherapist from Shrewsbury), Kevin Meacock, Mel Rees, Rob Turner (from Huddersfield), Lee Smelt, Mark Farrington (from Norwich), Paul McLoughlin, Jimmy Mullen (assistant manager). Front row: Tarki Micallef, Brian Flynn, John Carver (from Newcastle), Roger Gibbins, Jake King, Mike Ford, Nigel Vaughan, David Tong, Graham Withey.

David Giles (left) returned to City in early September 1985 after leaving Newport County. Since leaving Ninian Park in December 1978 he had played for Wrexham, Swansea City, Crystal Palace, Birmingham City and Wales. Meanwhile, forward Paul Wheeler (right) came from Aberaman as a non-contract player in mid-September 1985. The former Bristol Rovers apprentice was a caretaker at Cardiff College of Education in Cyncoed.

71

By mid-October 1985, City had won only two League games and were in the bottom three. This was one of those victories – 2-1 at Newport County on 26 August as Nigel Vaughan beats former County team-mate Mark Kendall for an injury-time winner.

On 9 October, Chris Marustik was signed from Swansea in exchange for Roger Gibbins. Here, he is celebrating a goal against Wigan ten days later with David Giles and a young Mike Ford (right), who had been signed in December 1984 after spells with Leicester and Devizes.

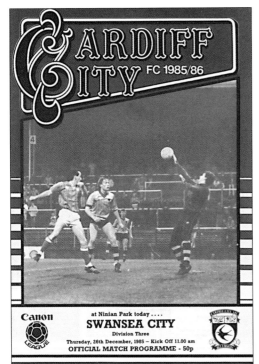

A local derby against Swansea City on 26 December 1985, but when this programme (left) was printed a few days later, Swansea had been wound-up in the High Court and it was uncertain if they would appear at Ninian Park. Playing for City in that match was defender Nigel Stevenson (right), who was in fact on loan from Swansea. He was to return to Ninian Park permanently in July 1987.

City beat Swansea 1-0 with this goal from Nigel Vaughan. The back-cladding of The Bob Bank had been taken down and the ground was becoming dilapidated as City struggled financially.

Two days later, on 28 December, City drew 1-1 at home with Newport County, both clubs in the bottom six of Division Three. Tarki Micallef, who had rejoined City in late September 1984 from Gillingham, beats his former Ninian Park team-mate Linden Jones.

Time was running out for City and so were visits to places like the Baseball Ground on 1 March 1986 when Derby were 2-1 winners in injury time. Lee Smelt punches clear watched by defender Phil Brignull, who was signed for £9,000 in a whip-round between directors and fans. City went down for the second consecutive year and Alan Durban lost his job.

Four

The Frank Burrows Era
1986-1990

In late April 1986, Tony Clemo (right), a local travel agent and a director for eleven years, agreed to take control of the club from Kenton Utilities and on 21 May appointed Sunderland coach Frank Burrows (left) as Cardiff City's manager.

Frank Burrows soon strengthened his backroom team by bringing in former Newport County manager Bobby Smith (left) as youth coach, while Jimmy Goodfellow (right) returned as trainer/physiotherapist after spells with Plymouth and Sunderland.

There were no fewer than seven new signings for 1986/87. This was the squad in mid-August 1986. From left to right, back row: Chris Marustik, Mike Ford, Andy Kerr (Shrewsbury), Alan Rogers (Southend), Graham Moseley (Brighton), Mel Rees, Rob Turner, Paul Wheeler, Steve Sherlock (Stockport), Phil Brignull. Front row: Nigel Vaughan, Paul Wimbleton (Portsmouth), Alan Curtis (Southampton), Terry Boyle (Newport County), Wayne Curtis, Jason Gummer, David Giles.

An amazing 5-4 home win over Plymouth on 26 August 1986 in a League Cup first round first leg match. City came from 4-1 down, with two goals from Nigel Vaughan, including this one.

City had a walkover into round three of the League Cup after Luton were thrown out of the competition for refusing to admit visiting fans. First Division Chelsea came to Ninian Park on 28 October and were beaten 2-1, with late September signing Nicky Platnauer getting both, including this header which levelled the score.

Another late September signing was forward Kevin Bartlett (left) from Fareham, seen here on his debut on 29 November challenging Cambridge United 'keeper Keith Branagan. City won 3-0 and Bartlett scored twice. Another new name was locally-born striker Chris Pike (right) on loan from Fulham, seen here making his City debut against Aldershot on 13 December 1986. He would be back permanently in July 1989.

City reached the FA Cup fourth round, losing 2-1 at Second Division Stoke City in front of 20,423. Here, Terry Boyle (second from left) has a shot blocked. City went on to finish thirteenth in Division Four and with hopes of better things to come.

City's squad for 1987/88, a great season that ended in promotion and a Welsh Cup win, included six summer signings. From left to right, back row: Jimmy Gilligan (Watford), Mike Ford, Paul Wheeler, Mark Kelly (Shrewsbury). Middle row: Steve Mardenborough, Nigel Stevenson (Swansea), Paul Sanderson (Halifax), Graham Moseley, John Roberts, Alan Curtis, Nicky Platnauer, Phil Bater (Brentford). Front row: Gareth Abraham, Jason Gummer, Paul Wimbleton, Terry Boyle (captain), Brian McDermott (Oxford Utd), Kevin Bartlett, Jason Perry.

Jimmy Gilligan was soon a regular scorer – this was his winner in the 1-0 home victory over Swansea City on 29 August 1987. After a later spell with Portsmouth, Gilligan became a Swansea player.

This was City's youth team which lost 1-0 at home to AFC Bournemouth in the FA Youth Cup first round on 11 November 1987. Five of the side (marked with an asterisk) would go on to play in the first team. From left to right, back row: Bob Smith (coach), Richard Haig, Alan Lewis*, Robert Jones, Morrys Scott*, Chris Fry*, Jason Leaman. Middle row: Robert Painter, Jonathan Morgan*, Jason Perry*, John Burrows, Jeff Dornan. Front row: Barry Hughes, Nicholas Denton, Paul Jarrett, 'Sandro Maladi.

About 4,000 City fans were amongst the 10,360 crowd at the Vetch Field on 1 January 1988 for a 2-2 draw, with Gilligan equalising in the last minute. Nicky Platnauer and former Swan Nigel Stevenson keep an eye on Joe Allon.

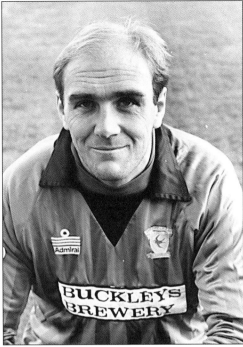

Welsh international striker Ian Walsh (left) came from Grimsby for £12,000 just before Christmas 1987, but was to be restricted through injury. Goalkeeper George Wood (right) came from Crystal Palace on loan in late January 1988 and was signed in July.

Nigel Stevenson scored just one goal that season; the opener against Newport County in a 4-0 home win on 4 April 1988. The Gwent side went out of the League at the end of that season.

One of the most vital results of the season when third-placed City beat fourth-placed Bolton 1-0 at Ninian Park on 15 April 1988 with this late goal from Jimmy Gilligan (right).

Alan Curtis had an outstanding season for City. Here, he is taking on Crewe's Maurice Doyle in the promotion-clinching home win on 5 May 1988. It was Alan's 500th League appearance.

The Crewe match was one of midfield player Mike Ford's last games for City. Ford (left) went to Oxford United for £150,000 at the end of the season, but would return a decade later.

Champagne in the dressing room after the win over Crewe in front of 10,125 spectators. City finished on a high, winning their last eight League and Welsh Cup matches.

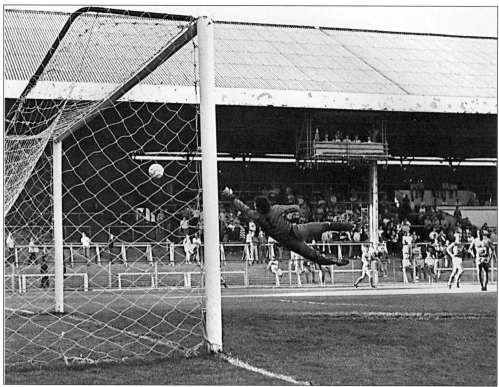

The goals which gave City a 2-0 Welsh Cup final win over Wrexham at the Vetch Field on 17 May 1988. *Above:* A tremendous left-footer from Alan Curtis beats Mike Salmon after thirteen minutes. *Below:* Kevin Bartlett heads on a Brian McDermott corner for Jimmy Gilligan (left) to score after thirty-four minutes.

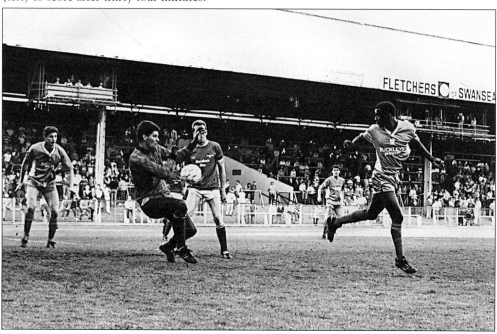

The team and their fans celebrate a League and cup double after the win over Wrexham and there is satisfaction for manager Frank Burrows and chairman Tony Clemo. Could City build on their success?

FA of Wales assistant-secretary Eddie Harrison (left) was appointed City's secretary in the summer of 1988, following the departure of Ron Jones to Portsmouth. Eddie stayed until October 1991, when he joined Chesterfield. Also arriving at Ninian Park was West Bromwich Albion winger Steve Lynex (right) who became known to City's fans as 'Lethal' Lynex.

A disappointing start for City with a 2-1 home defeat by Fulham on 27 August 1988. Ian Walsh (right), who scored in that game, is challenged by Fulham's Jeff Eckhardt (with long hair), who was to join City from Stockport eight years later.

City were back in the Cup Winners' Cup with a first round first leg trip to Irish club Derry City on 7 September 1988. *Above:* Wimbleton, Wood, Lynex, Gummer, Tupling, Bartlett and McDermott in relaxed mood the night before the game. *Below:* Frank Burrows discusses the prospects with *Echo* football correspondent Robert Phillips.

Above: Terry Boyle and Jimmy Gilligan challenge the Derry defence for a free-kick in a 0-0 draw before a capacity 10,500 Brandywell crowd. *Below:* No problems for City in the second leg on 5 October with a 4-0 win. Jimmy Gilligan couldn't miss this one and went on to score a hat-trick.

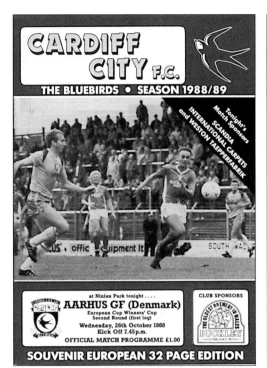

In round two, City played Danish side Aarhus. *Left:* The programme cover for the home leg played on 28 October 1988. *Right:* Kevin Bartlett gets in a shot during the first leg at Ninian Park, which City lost 2-1. Aarhus won the second leg 4-0. Bartlett went to West Bromwich in mid-February 1989 for £100,000 when City's finances were in trouble.

A 2-2 draw against Swansea City on 26 December 1988 in front of a 10,635 Ninian Park crowd, with two for Jimmy Gilligan. This was his first, watched by Robbie James and Alan Knill (both later to play for City), and Andy Melville. City finished sixteenth in Division Three, just three points clear of relegation.

Frank Burrows left for Portsmouth on 28 August 1989 after City had lost their opening three Third Division and League Cup games without scoring. Len Ashurst, who had been assisting Blackpool, was reappointed three days later, and watches his first home game against Brentford on 2 September.

Chris Pike (left) was a July 1989 signing from Fulham, while Colin Griffith (right) cost £60,000 from Kettering on 3 October. They are in action during Griffith's debut at Huddersfield on 7 October with Griffith having just scored in City's 3-2 win. Pike scored Cardiff's other two goals in the game.

Two others who came in 1989/90 were full-back Ray Daniel (left), a £40,000 signing from Hull in late July, and goalkeeper Roger Hansbury (right), who was on loan from Birmingham City in mid-October, and signed for £15,000 just before Christmas 1989.

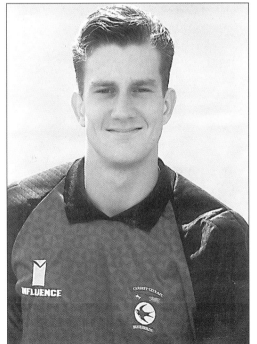 

Two early October 1989 signings were former West Bromwich Albion reserve 'keeper Gavin Ward (left) and Swindon midfielder Leigh Barnard (right) who cost £25,000.

City signed winger Jeff Chandler from Bolton on 1 November 1989 for £15,000. He can be seen in this team group from late November. From left to right, back row: Jimmy Goodfellow (physiotherapist/coach), Richard Haig, Gareth Abraham, Morrys Scott, George Wood, Pat O'Hagan, Chris Pike, Roger Gibbins, Jeff Chandler, Leigh Barnard. Front row: Jon Morgan, Chris Fry, Steve Lynex, Ray Daniel, Tony Clemo (chairman), Ian Rodgerson (captain), Len Ashurst (manager), Cohen Griffith, Mark Kelly, Damon Searle, Jason Perry.

One of the highlights of what would be a relegation season, the 1-0 win at Swansea on 26 December 1989. Leigh Barnard, who scored the goal, gets away from Keith Walker in front of a 12,244 attendance.

City reached the FA Cup third round and played QPR in a 0-0 draw at Ninian Park, seen by 13,834. Cohen Griffith is challenged by Danny Maddix (right). The £50,000-plus gate receipts were stolen from Ninian Park that weekend. It was found to be an inside job perpetrated by one of the matchday staff. City lost the replay 2-0.

On 13 January 1990, fourteen-year-old Scott Young from the Rhondda signed Associate Schoolboy forms, watched by his parents and chairman Tony Clemo. Scott signed professional four years later and in the year 2000 was the club's longest-serving player.

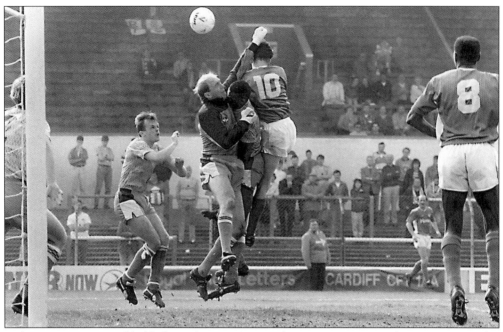

A disappointing second half of 1989/90 saw City go down just two years after promotion. This was a 2-2 home draw against Blackpool on 31 March in front of less than 3,000 fans. George Wood (on loan to Blackpool from City) punches clear from Jason Perry (10).

Left: At least groundsman Wayne Nash had a boost when he and his assistant were presented with a seed spreader by Adar Glas Supporters Club secretary Mair Daniel in late April 1990. *Right:* In the final game of 1989/90 at Bury, eighteen-year-old YTS player Nathan Blake (right) made his sixth appearance of the season. The former Newport County and Chelsea junior would sign professional forms in the summer and play a major part in City's recovery.

Five

Wright is Watching Us
1990-1993

Into Division Four for 1990/91 with three newcomers and five ex-YTS players who had become professionals in July 1990. From left to right, back row: Ian Rodgerson, Nathan Blake (ex-YTS), Alan Lewis, Roger Hansbury, Gavin Ward, Gareth Abraham, Chris Pike. Middle row: Jimmy Goodfellow (physiotherapist/coach), Neil Matthews (Blackpool), Stephen Hookings (ex-YTS), Jason Perry, Jon Morgan, Chris Fry, Damon Searle (ex-YTS), Chris Summers (ex-YTS), Pat Heard (Rotherham), Gavin Tait (Youth Development Officer). Front row: Jeff Chandler, Lee Stephens (ex-YTS), Cohen Griffith, Len Ashurst (manager), Roger Gibbins, Tony Clemo (chairman), Mark Jones (Swindon), Leigh Barnard, Ray Daniel.

Left: In August 1990, Dr Leslie Hamilton (left) had reached twenty-five-years as the club's medical officer. The Cardiff medical practitioner had been appointed by Jimmy Scoular in August 1965 and was connected with the club until he died in early June 2000. *Right:* It was a good start to the season for Cohen Griffith (right) as he scored in this 3-3 home draw with Torquay to make it five goals in the first five League and Cup games.

Defender Jason Perry, with chairman Tony Clemo, is presented by Mr Grant Walshe (Barclays Bank), with his Barclays Young Eagle of the Month Award (Wales and the West) before the 1-1 home draw with Peterborough on 27 October. Jason had made his debut in March 1987 before he was seventeen.

A shock against Vauxhall Conference club Merthyr Tydfil in the Welsh Cup with a 4 -1 home defeat in round three on 6 November 1990. Nathan Blake gets in a header.

An even bigger shock in mid-November as City are held 0-0 at home in the FA Cup first round by Isthmian League side Hayes. Nathan Blake sees his shot blocked by 'keeper Paul Hyde. Hayes won the replay 1-0 at Brentford's ground.

Former City managers and players turned up on Sunday 2 December 1990 for a celebrities' match in aid of long-serving kit manager Harry Parsons' Testimonial Fund. Here, Harry Parsons meets Jimmy Scoular watched by (from right): Jimmy Andrews, 'referee' Ronnie Bird (with refreshment), City patron Norman 'Hunter' Phillips and former England international Terry Cooper.

Left: The usual questionable banter between old friends Harry Parsons and Phil Dwyer. *Right:* Harry finds a suitable shirt for youth team coach Eddie May, who would be in charge of the first team the following season.

In late March 1991, as City vainly tried to close the gap on the play-off places, three players were bought in. Their wages were funded by Barry holiday centre owner Rick Wright, who had become involved with the club. Defender Ken De Mange (left), on loan from Hull for the second time that season, and midfielder Kevin MacDonald (right), on loan from Coventry City, are both seen here playing against Northampton at Ninian Park on 1 April. Phil Heath was also signed from Oxford United.

Former youth team coach Eddie May took charge of the first team's affairs on 11 July 1991 following Len Ashurst's late May departure. One of Eddie's vital signings was midfielder Paul Ramsey from Leicester City for £40,000 on 22 August.

A few days before the Ramsey deal, Eddie signed midfielder Paul Millar (left) for £60,000 from Port Vale and striker Carl Dale (right), who cost £95,000 from Chester City. Both fees were provided by Rick Wright. They are seen in action against Carlisle in a 1-0 home win on 31 August 1991.

On 1 September 1991, Eddie May, together with chairman Tony Clemo and his wife Lynda, visited City's oldest fan Mrs Ida Lewis, who was 100 years old that day. Mrs Lewis was the daughter of City's 1927 cup winning chairman Walter Parker. Also present was Mrs Lewis's son Bill, who is holding a photograph of his grandfather and himself in the FA Cup as a baby.

Rick Wright was now officially titled the club's 'Financial Controller'. Here he is before the home match with Rochdale on 7 September 1991 with match guests Robbie Regan (left), the ex-British Flyweight Champion, and his manager Dai Gardner.

Left: A good pedigree – Cameron Toshack, son of former City striker John Toshack, makes his debut as a substitute in this 2-1 home win over Scarborough on 21 September. *Right:* City's best result of the season came on 5 October, with a 5-0 home win over Wrexham. Here, Chris Pike beats defender Nigel Beaumont to score his hat-trick.

Left: Young and old in late November 1991 as Lee Baddeley, watched by 1927 hero Ernie Curtis, begins work on the demolition of the enclosure to convert it into an all-seated area. *Right:* In mid-December, John Williams initially signs on loan from AFC Bournemouth, welcomed by Tony Clemo and Eddie May on a frosty day.

Chris Pike scored a hat-trick in this 3-3 home draw against Stourbridge in the fourth round of the Welsh Cup on 7 December 1991. He had now scored 13 League and cup goals while co-striker Carl Dale had 11.

The new enclosure was first used for the visit of Maidstone United on 1 January 1992, with women and children admitted free, and male adults for just £3.00. Rick Wright (below) was in his element. An 8,023 crowd turned up, but City lost 5-0, their heaviest home defeat in fourteen years.

Two good midfield loan signings on 22 January 1992: Eddie Newton (left) from Chelsea and Gerry Harrison (right) from Bristol City.

Newton (6) scores his first City goal with the winner in a 3-2 home victory over Mansfield on a foggy Friday night on 31 January 1992.

City now had a useful-looking line-up and were in the top eight of Division Four. This was the squad in early February 1992. From left to right, back row: Jamie Unsworth, Pat Heard, Jason Perry, Damon Searle, Paul Ramsey, Andy Gorman, Robin Semark. Middle row: Neil Matthews, Lee Baddeley, Chris Pike, John Williams, Roger Hansbury, Gavin Ward, Gareth Abraham, Cameron Toshack, Allan Lewis, Paul Millar. Bottom row: Cohen Griffith, Nathan Blake, Carl Dale, Eddie May (team manager), Roger Gibbins (captain), Eddie Newton, Gerry Harrison.

It was a big occasion at Ninian Park on 29 February 1992 when leaders Burnley played fifth-placed City and the club's official history publication by John Crooks was launched in the presence of former players and managers. From left to right: Ken Hollyman, Jimmy Andrews, Arthur 'Buller' Lever, Jimmy Scoular, Don Murray, Colin Baker, Ted Gorin, Ernie Curtis.

There were 16,030 at the game against Burnley – City's biggest crowd in nearly twelve years. Burnley, managed by former City defender Jimmy Mullen, scored twice in the last five minutes to win 2-0 after Gerry Harrison (below) had gone near to giving City the lead.

The rough and the smooth! City's Jason Perry, Roger Gibbins, Damon Searle and Paul Miller went along to the Essanelle salon in David Morgan and Co. for a facial and trim followed by a visit to the casuals department. They are seen here before (left) and after (right).

Two March 1992 signings: midfielder Gary Gill (left), a free transfer from Darlington, and defender Gary Bellamy (right), on loan from Wolves.

Left-side midfielder or winger Alan Walsh, once of Bristol City, came as a non-contract player in March 1992 after his return from Turkish side Besiktas, but only stayed for the rest of that season.

In late March 1992, Beryl Taylor, one of City's best-known supporters, died at the age of sixty. She had followed the club since 1946 and always stood in the same spot at every home match – behind the visiting team's dugout next to the players' tunnel. Beryl was known to generations of City players, many of whom would acknowledge her as they came onto the pitch, usually receiving a packet of chewing gum from her.

The 4-0 home win over Halifax on 11 April saw two goals for Carl Dale to make it 26 in League and cup matches. He went on to score 29 in his first season with City.

It was a great result for eleven-year-old junior Bluebird Daniel Sheppeard, who had won a competition to be City's 'Manager for the Day'. Here is Daniel, watched by his co-manager Eddie May, giving his post-match views to *Echo* correspondent Robert Phillips.

Eddie Newton's final home game for City before going back to Chelsea – a 3-1 win over Barnet on 20 April 1992 when he scored. At the end of the match he was carried off in triumph by delighted City fans, but he never returned and City just missed the play-offs.

Above: A great night for loyal Harry Parsons on 5 May 1992 when 11,070 – the best crowd of the season – saw his testimonial match against Tottenham. *Below:* Two nights later at the National Stadium, Harry held the Welsh Cup after City's 1-0 victory over Hednesford Town.

Ninian Park was assuming a new look by early August 1992. The main stand enclosure (above) now had an extended roof cover, while the Bob Bank (below) upper section was now a seated area.

Four new signings in the summer of 1992 for what would be a Third (previously Fourth) Division Championship and Welsh Cup winning season. From left to right, back row: Lee Baddeley, Chris Pike, Gareth Abraham, Paul Millar, Derek Brazil (Manchester United). Middle row: Jason Donovan, Robbie James (Bradford City), Jason Perry, Gavin Ward, Mark Grew (Port Vale), Allan Lewis, Nicky Richardson (Halifax), Paul Ramsey. Front row: Cohen Griffith, Damon Searle, Roger Gibbins, Eddie May (team manager), John Williams, Carl Dale, Nathan Blake.

Paul Ramsey (left), with the Welsh Cup, leads out City against Darlington on 15 August 1992, but despite the efforts of Chris Pike (right) it was a disappointing 0-0 draw in front of 8,399.

Damon Searle, now in his third year as a full professional, was to have an outstanding season, being ever-present in 1992/93. Here he is against Carlisle United in a 2-2 home draw on 8 September.

Austrian club Baumit Admira Wacker were at Ninian Park on 16 September 1992 for a European Cup Winners' Cup first round first leg. Injuries, suspensions and the rule limiting teams to three foreigners meant a reshuffled City side with Tony Bird (2) in attack, seen here with Paul Ramsey in a 1-1 draw. City lost the second leg 2-0.

Financial controller Rick Wright (left) took over the club from Tony Clemo in May 1992. Here he is presenting 1991/92 Wales under-21 caps to Damon Searle, Nathan Blake and Jason Perry before the 1-1 home draw with Rochdale on 3 October 1992. Club secretary Jim Finney is on the right.

'Our house' – it's a tight fit for Eddie May, Chris Pike and Jimmy Goodfellow at Ton Pentre on 27 October for a 2-0 Welsh Cup third round win.

Paul Ramsey seals the 2-0 win at Ton Pentre from the penalty spot against the backdrop of an old colliery slag heap, a reminder of City's early professional days from 1910 to 1912, when they were regular visitors to Ynys Park.

Tony Kelly (8), on a month's loan from Stoke City, beats Scunthorpe's Mark Samways at Ninian Park on 31 October 1992 to score on his debut in a 3-0 win.

Nathan Blake goes near against Bath City at Ninian Park on 14 November 1992 in the FA Cup first round, but not near enough. City lost 3-2 against the Conference club in one of the major shocks of the season.

A Baltimore (USA) policewoman on an exchange visit watched the game. Her South Wales police colleague did his best to explain what was happening!

On 28 November 1992, before the 3-0 home win over Bury, there was a tribute to Ernie Curtis, the last survivor of City's 1927 FA Cup winning team, who had died aged eighty-five, seven days earlier. From left to right: Cohen Griffith, Chris Pike, Steve McRaye (reserve coach), Eddie May, Jimmy Goodfellow, Wayne Nash (groundsman).

Striker Phil Stant (left) was signed from Mansfield for £100,000 in early December 1992, scoring on his 8 December debut against Hereford in a 3-2 Autoglass Trophy home win. However, Carl Dale (right) suffered a long-term knee injury against Wrexham ten days later, so Chris Pike (on his left) was to form an attacking partnership with Stant.

A sensational City signing on 5 January 1993. The former Everton and Wales captain Kevin Ratcliffe, released by the Merseyside club on 31 December, came to Ninian Park on a non-contract match-by-match arrangement for the rest of the season and team manager Eddie May was delighted. Ratcliffe marked his City debut four days later at Carlisle United by heading the winner in a 2-1 victory and was to prove inspirational in the promotion success that season.

Nathan Blake and Damon Searle acclaim a Blake goal in January 1993. Newport-born Nathan was the nephew of the legendary Great Britain Rugby League captain Clive Sullivan. The former Newport County and Chelsea junior, who joined City as a YTS player in 1989/90, made his debut at left-back against Bristol Rovers at Twerton Park on 24 March 1990 and later played in various positions for Cardiff City. The talented Blake was transferred to Sheffield United on 17 February 1994 for £300,000 with an extra £200,000 if United stayed in the Premiership – which they didn't!

You couldn't stop Phil Stant celebrating when he scored. *Above:* The former soldier is collared by Jason Perry after netting one of his three goals in the 4-0 Welsh Cup fifth round home win over Maesteg Park on 16 January 1993. *Below:* In action against Swansea's Keith Walker three days later at Ninian Park when the two clubs met in the Autoglass Trophy.

Sutton Coldfield-born goalkeeper Gavin Ward had gained a regular place in mid-October 1992, retaining it for the rest of the season. Gavin had originally joined the club on trial in early October 1989, after being released by West Bromwich, and had been signed as a professional by City in early December 1989, making his debut later that month in a Leyland Daf Cup preliminary round 4-0 defeat at Shrewsbury. His League debut came in mid-September 1991 at Blackpool. He was transferred to Leicester City in the summer of 1993 for £175,000 and was later with Bolton and Stoke City.

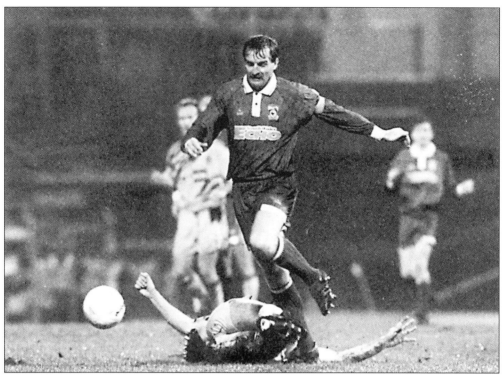

In the Autoglass Trophy second round, City met Swansea at Ninian Park, losing 2-1 in front of 13,516 – up to this time the biggest-ever crowd in the competition, apart from the final. *Above:* Robbie James in action against his old club. *Below:* Kevin Ratcliffe, supported by Phil Stant (left), battles his way through.

Thirty-seven-year-old Robbie James receives his Man of the Match award from Wales team manager Terry Yorath after the Autoglass Trophy game against Swansea City. A veteran of twenty-one seasons of League football, Robbie had played for Swansea, QPR, Stoke, Leicester City, Bradford City and Wales before arriving at Ninian Park in mid-August 1992 for a £17,500 transfer tribunal fee. A midfield player for most of his career, he had an outstanding 1992/93 season at right-back for City and was Player of the Year. In October 1993 he joined Merthyr as player-manager and was in the same role at Llanelli when he collapsed and died on the pitch from a heart attack on 18 February 1998.

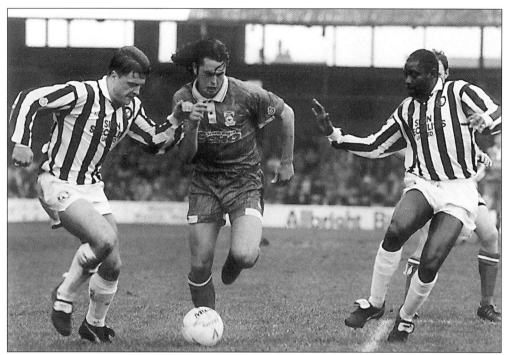

Midfielder Nicky Richardson missed only three League games that season and proved a good signing. Here he is against Walsall in a 2-1 home win on 30 January 1993.

City won all six League games in January 1993 and Eddie May was named Third Division Manager of the Month. He receives his award from Graham Couch of Barclays Bank before the 4-0 home win over Torquay on 13 February.

On 27 February 1993, City had to beat Crewe at Ninian Park to equal the 1946/47 side's record of nine consecutive League wins. Ken Hollyman, Fred Stansfield and Arthur Lever (with secretary Jim Finney on left), stars from the 1946/47 side, were there to see it. Their record was safe, though, as City drew 1-1.

Promotion was achieved on 24 April 1993 without City in action. Others results went their way and Rick Wright and Eddie May celebrated with fans at the City versus Plymouth reserve game, when 3,000 turned up. Wright had invited junior Bluebirds to make their mothers 'Directors for a Day'!

With promotion secured, a 17,253 Ninian Park crowd saw City go top of the table on 1 May 1993 with this 2-1 win over Shrewsbury Town. A rare goal from Jason Perry, heading in a Nathan Blake free-kick, gives City a thirty-fifth minute lead.

The title was won at Scunthorpe with a 3-0 victory on 8 May 1993 when some 5,000 City fans were in the 7,407 Glanford Park attendance. Cohen Griffith races past Scunthorpe full-back Joe Joyce.

Phil Stant, who scored a hat-trick in the Welsh Cup final at the National Stadium against Rhyl to make it 19 League and cup goals since his December arrival, holds the cup aloft, watched by Jason Perry, Carl Dale and Cohen Griffith. Rick Wright looks satisfied.

The end of a great season: the Third Division title, the Welsh Cup, a resurgence in support and a place in Europe. Rick Wright had achieved his target, but would he and City take it on from here?